Introducing The Positions...

for VIOLA—Vol. II SECOND, FOURTH and FIFTH POSITIONS

There are many students today, who, after an elementary training on the viola, restricted entirely to the *first* position of their instrument, find themselves unable to participate in the activities of amateur orchestras and ensembles, due to their inability to play in the higher positions of their instrument. Neither can they perform much in the way of available solo literature, due to their limited technic. From a practical standpoint, there are *five* higher positions on the viola, in addition to a so-called *half* position, which is sometimes referred to as the "saddle" or "nut" position.

INTRODUCING THE POSITIONS for Viola, Volume One, takes up the study of the *third* position, followed by the *half* position. The *third* position should at all times be given first consideration, for not only is it the easiest to play of all the higher positions (due to the convenience afforded in resting the left hand against the edge of the instrument), but also it is used more in actual performance than any of the other higher positions. By going directly from the *first* to the *third* position, students learn to play positions in the exact manner in which they will use them most frequently. Furthermore, when following the procedure of taking up the *third* position before the *second* position, students are given an early opportunity to begin the very important study of shifting, which unfortunately, is neglected in nearly all viola methods dealing with position study in the traditional manner. Following the

study of the *third* position, the next position to be taken up in relative importance, is the *half* position. Students who follow the system of alternate fingerings offered by this position are able to simplify many complicated passages and avoid awkward stretches of the fingers, especially when playing in sharp keys.

INTRODUCING THE POSITIONS for Viola, Volume Two, is a continuation of the course of study presented in Volume One, and includes the study of the *second, fourth* and *fifth* positions, as well as the introduction of the treble clef, which is used frequently in viola music to avoid the use of innumerable ledger lines when extremely high notes are employed.

INTRODUCING THE POSITIONS for Viola, Volumes One and Two, constitute together, an introductory course of position playing for the viola. For additional material of a more advanced nature, the famous viola school by Ritter, and the equally famous method of Cavallini, are recommended, as well as the many excellent etudes of Hoffmeister, Bruni, Blumenstengel, Palaschko, Schoen, Campagnoli, Kreutzer, Fiorillo, Rode, and others. In addition, the orchestral works of Wagner, Richard Strauss, Berlioz, and similar operatic and symphonic composers may be used. From these sources a wealth of advanced material utilizing higher positions on the viola is available.

Harvey S. Whistler, Ph. D.

The Second Position

This position is NOT to be studied until the player has completed all of the third position and half position studies presented in "Introducing the Positions, for Viola, Vol. I."

Preparatory Studies in the Key of F Major

⌐¬ = Half-step; fingers close together

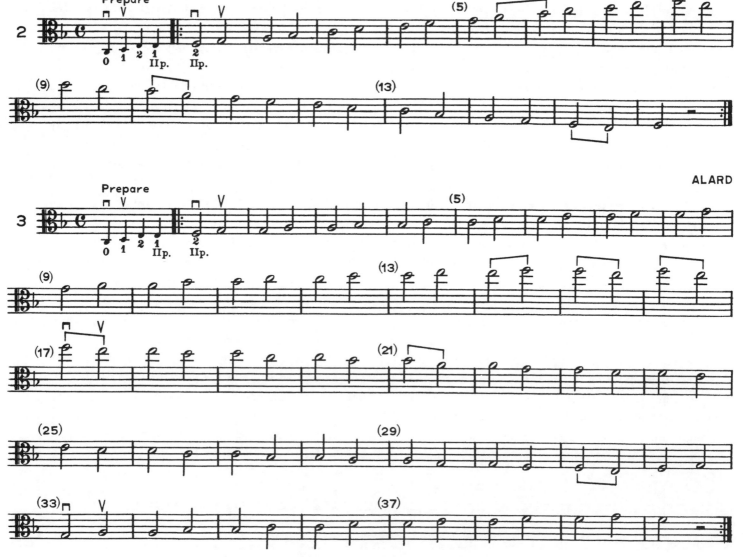

In playing positions, do not employ open A, D or G strings unless fingering is so marked.

Selected Studies in the Second Position

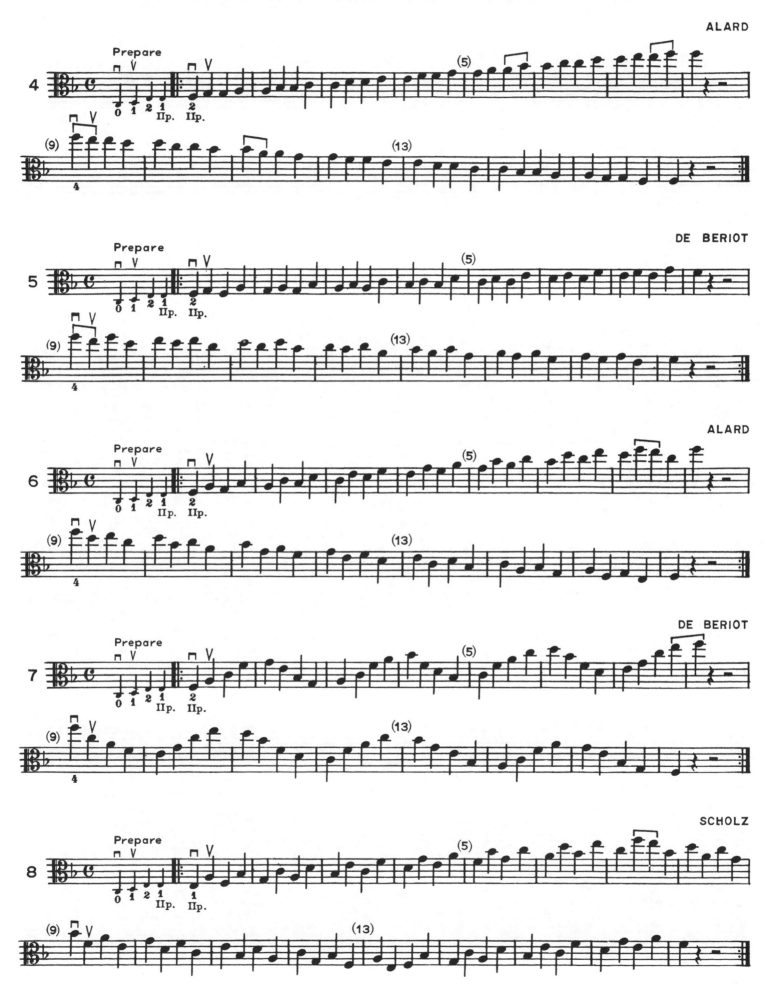

Exercise

HERMANN

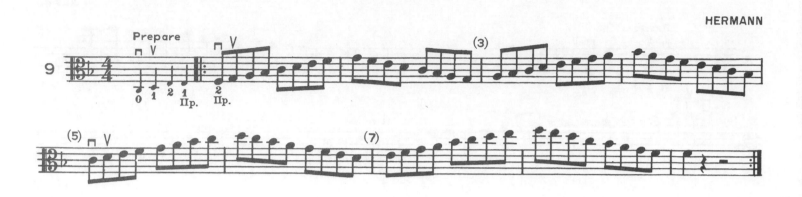

Foundation Study

DANCLA

Etude in F

SITT

Key of B♭ Major

Etude

SCHOLZ

Also practice (1) slurring each four tones, and (2) slurring each complete measure.

* $\underset{\smile}{1}$ = Draw back first finger while hand remains in same position.

Key of E♭ Major

Etude

SITT

Advanced Etude in the Second Position
(Based on a Rode Caprice)

RODE

(Remain in second position throughout.)

Shifting from First to Second Position

When shifting from the first to a higher position, do not take the finger up and put it down again; instead, *slide* into the higher position.

Shifting from One Finger to Another

The student should shift forward on the finger that was last down, and likewise, shift backward on the finger that was last down.

The small notes in the exercises below indicate the movement of the fingers in shifting, and as the student perfects his ability to shift from one note to another, the small notes eventually should not be heard.

A String

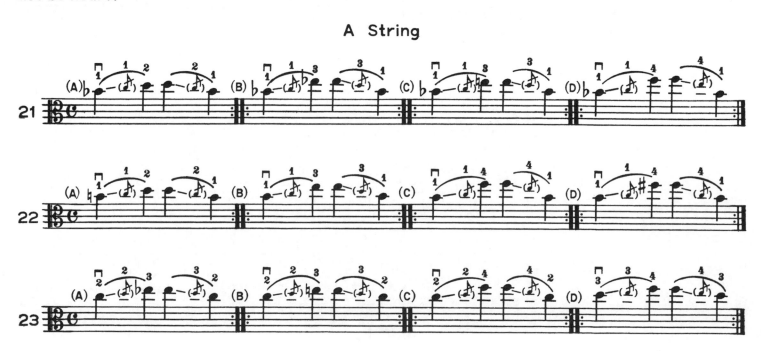

D String

G String

C String

Etude in the First, Second and Third Positions

Also practice slowly, using a separate bow for each tone.

SITT

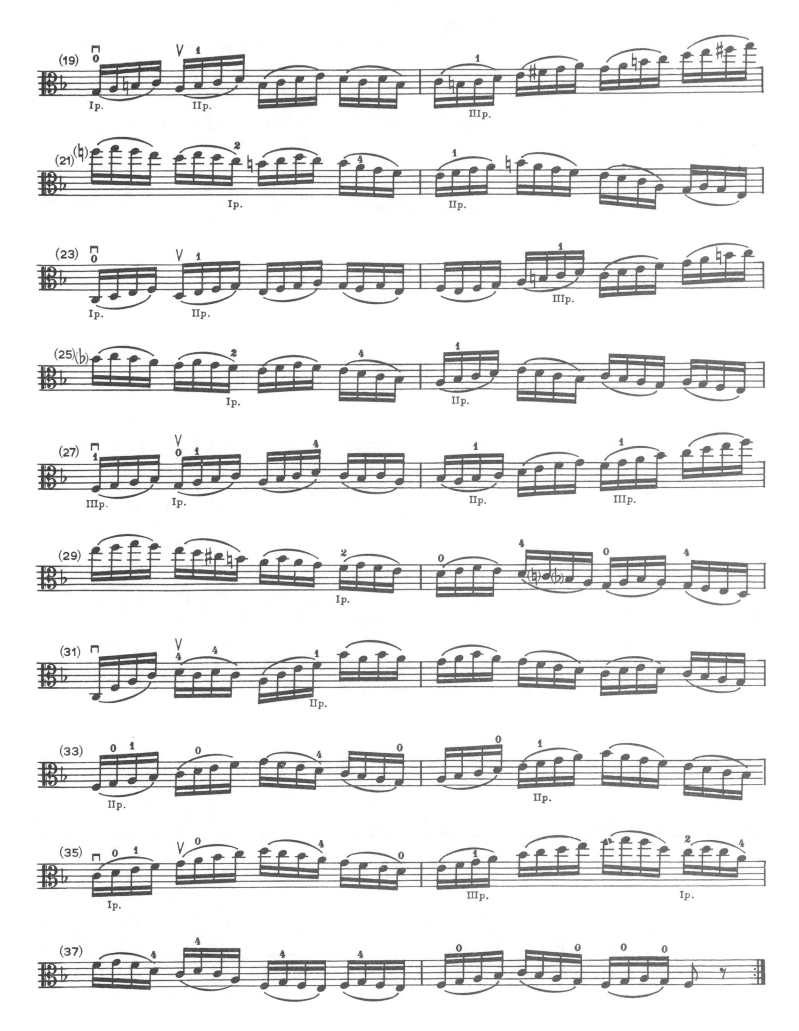

Adagio Élégiaque
(Duet in the First and Second Positions)

RIES
Transcribed by
H. A. Hummel

The Fourth Position

Preparatory Studies in the Key of F Major

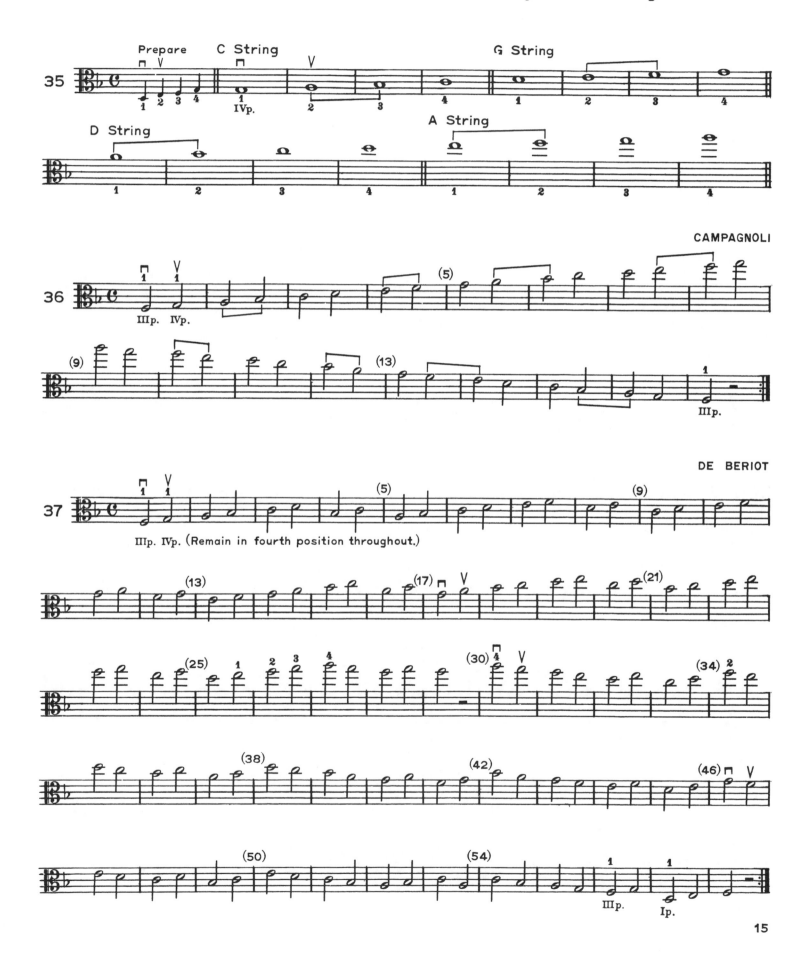

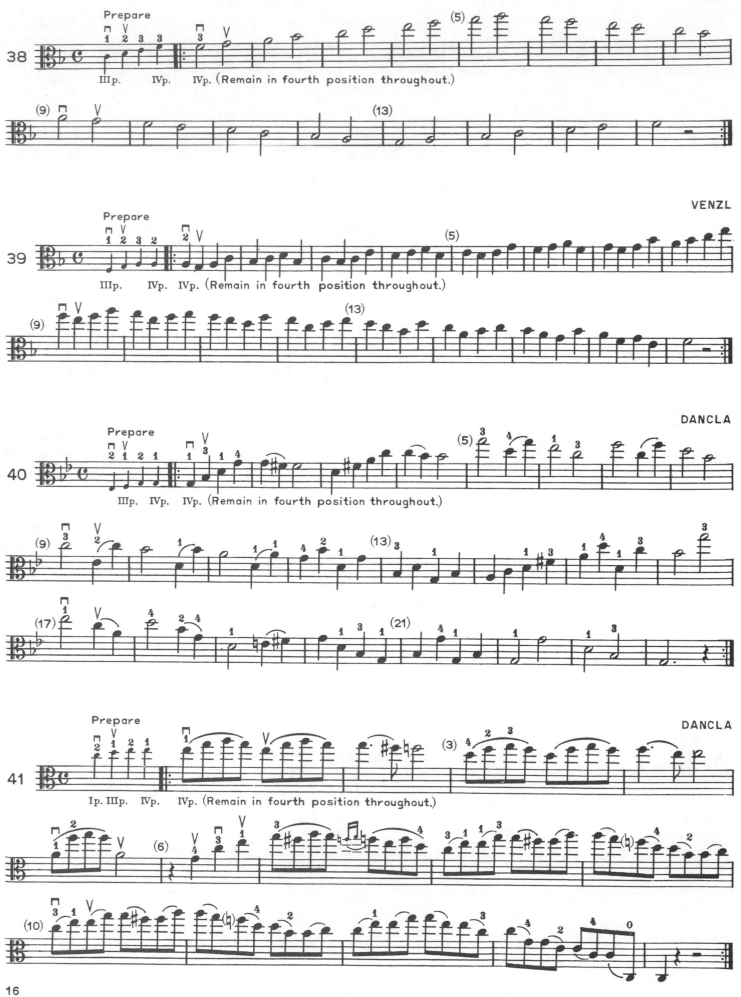

From Alto to Treble Clef

If difficulty is encountered in reading from treble clef, the performer should turn to "Modern Hohmann-Wohlfahrt Beginning Method for Violin, Vol. I," by Harvey S. Whistler, and play in the first position, all studies and pieces that require only the A, D, and G strings. The remaining material in this volume may be played on the viola by utilizing the higher positions.

TREBLE CLEF NOTATION AND FINGERING

First Position

Second Position

Third Position

Fourth Position

High Tones in the Fourth Position
(Alto and Treble Clefs)

RITTER

Technic Builders in the Fourth Position
(Alto and Treble Clefs)

RITTER

Extending Fourth Finger in Fourth Position
$\widehat{4}$ = Extend fourth finger while hand remains in same position

CAMPAGNOLI

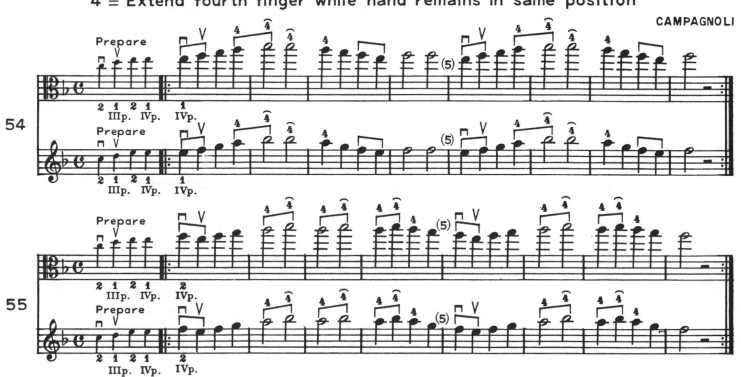

Key of B♭ Major

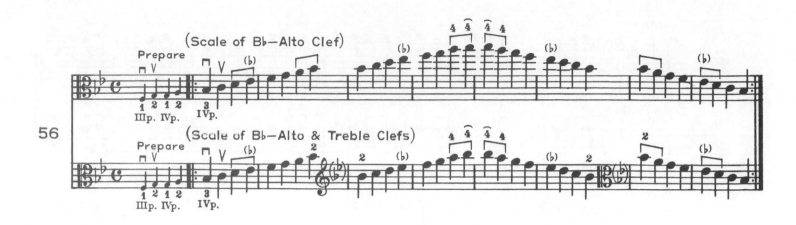

Etude

DANCLA

* While extending 4th finger, be sure to keep hand in same position.

Key of C Major

Etude

Also practice slowly, using a separate bow for each tone.

RIES

*1 = While drawing back 1st finger, be sure to keep hand in same position.

Key of G Major

(Scale of G - Alto Clef)

(Scale of G - Alto & Treble Clefs)

60

Etude

Also practice slowly, using a separate bow for each tone.

SITT

61

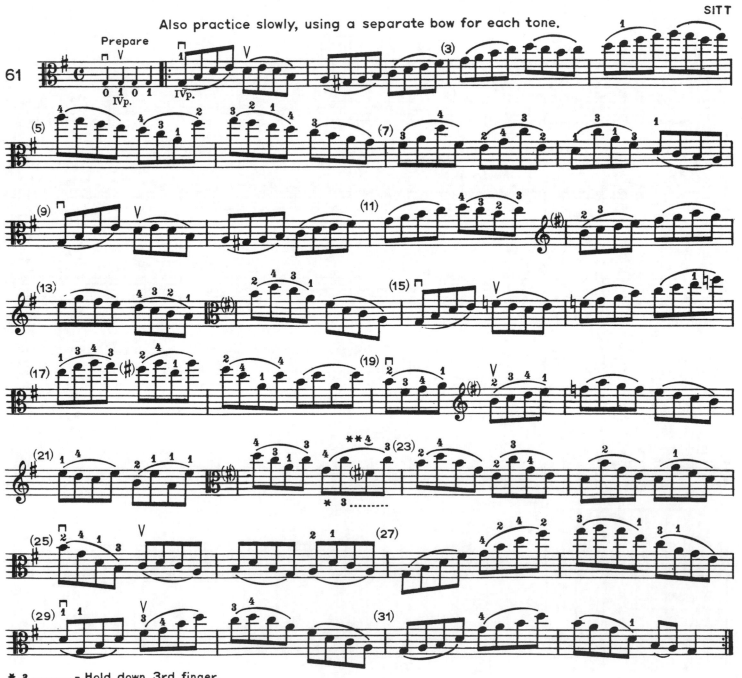

* 3 .... = Hold down 3rd finger.

* 4 = Draw back 4th finger while 3rd finger is held down in same position on adjoining string

22

Key of D Major

Etude

SITT

Key of E♭ Major

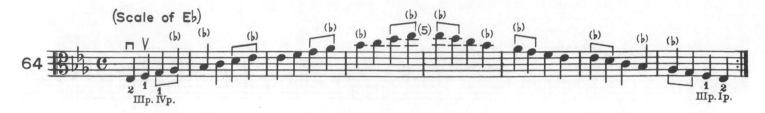

(Scale of E♭)

Etude

Also practice slowly, using a separate bow for each tone.

RIES

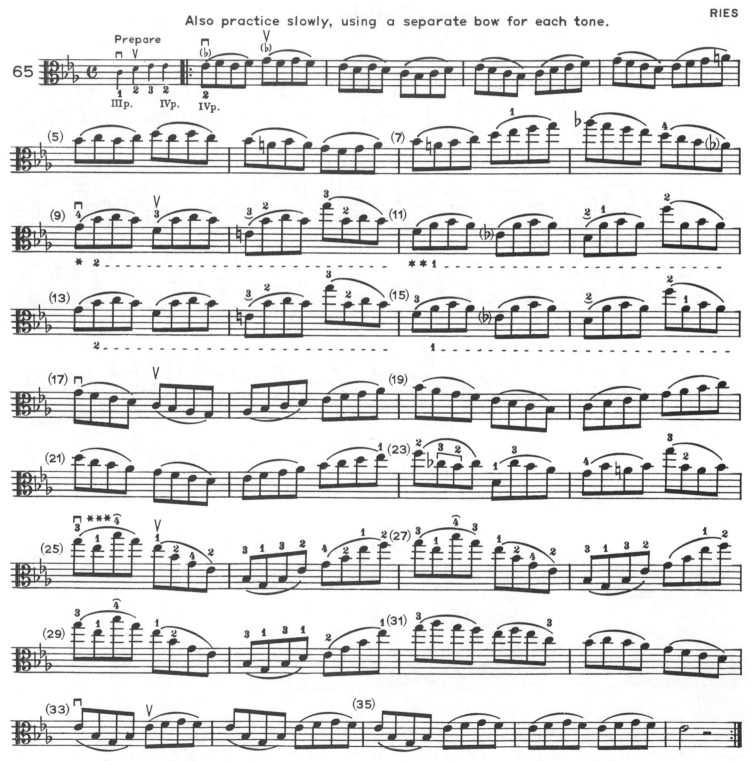

* 2 _ _ _ _ = Hold down 2nd finger.

** 1 _ _ _ _ = Hold down 1st finger.

*** While extending 4th finger, be sure to keep hand in same position.

Valse de Salon
(Duet in the Fourth Position)

ALARD
Tanscribed by
H. A. Hummel

Shifting to the Fourth Position

The student must remember that in shifting from one position to another he is NOT to take the finger up and put it down again; instead he is to *slide* into the higher position.

From Third to Fourth Position

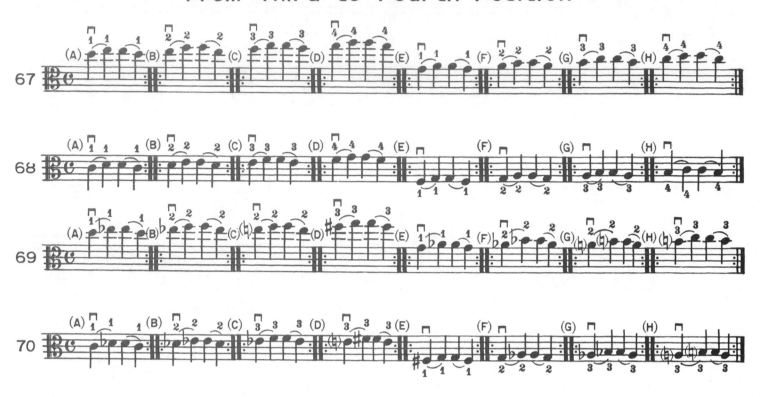

From Second to Fourth Position

From First to Fourth Position

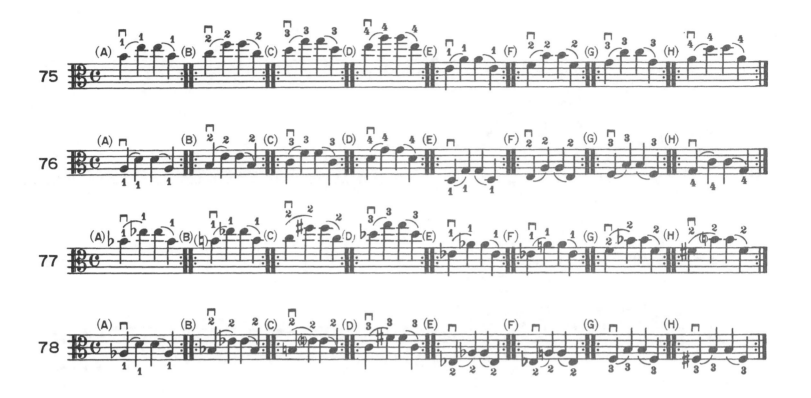

Shifting from One Finger to Another

The student must remember to shift forward on the finger that was last down, and likewise shift backward on the finger that was last down. The student also must remember that the small notes in the exercises below merely indicate the movements of the fingers in shifting, and as the ability to shift from one note to another is perfected, the small notes eventually must not be heard.

Etude in the Second and Fourth Positions

SCHOEN

* While extending 4th finger, be sure to keep hand in same position.

28

The Fifth Position

Preparatory Studies in the Key of F Major

The fingering of the fifth position is the same as the fingering of the first position (i. e., identical notes require the same fingers), only a string lower, and at a higher place on the fingerboard.

The nearer the strings are to the bridge of the viola, the higher they lie above the finger-board; as a result, when playing in the fifth position, it is essential that the strings are pressed down more forcibly than when playing in lower positions.

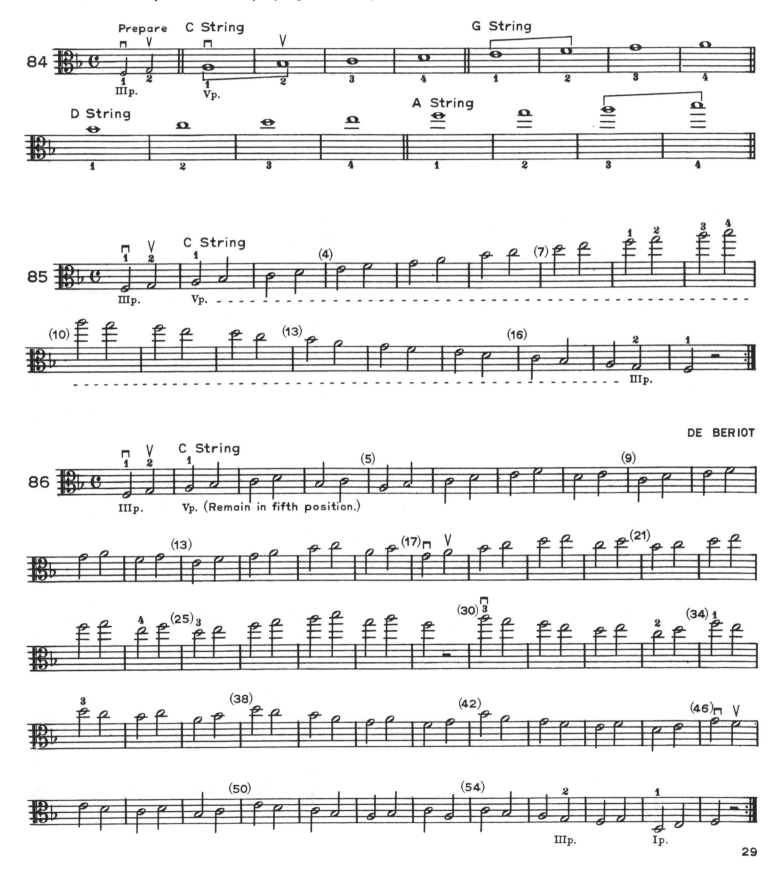

DE BERIOT

High Tones in the Fifth Position
(Alto and Treble Clefs)

RITTER

Technic Builders in the Fifth Position
(Alto and Treble Clefs)

RITTER

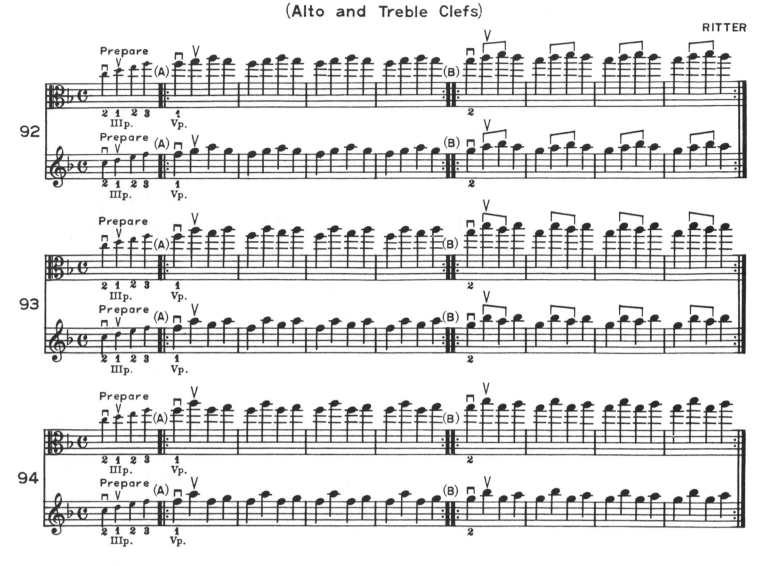

Extending Fourth Finger in Fifth Position

While extending 4th finger, remember to keep hand in same position.

CAMPAGNOLI

Selected Studies in the Fifth Position
(Alto Clef)

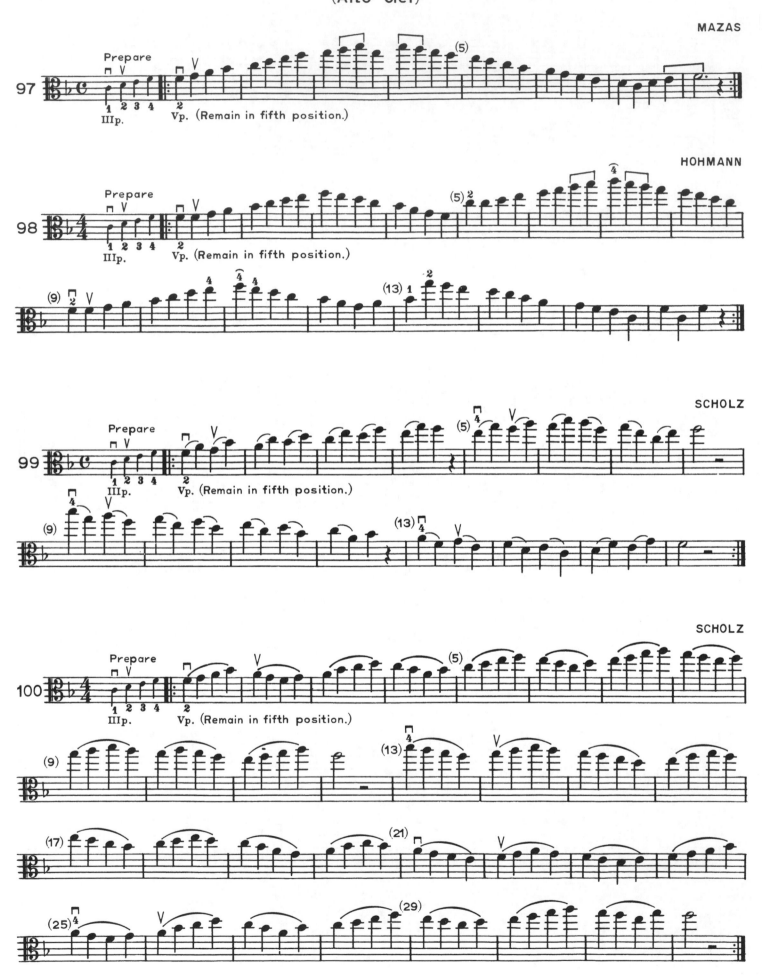

Selected Studies in the Fifth Position
(Treble Clef)

MAZAS

HOHMANN

SCHOLZ

SCHOLZ

Fifth Position Etude in F Major
(Alto Clef)

SITT

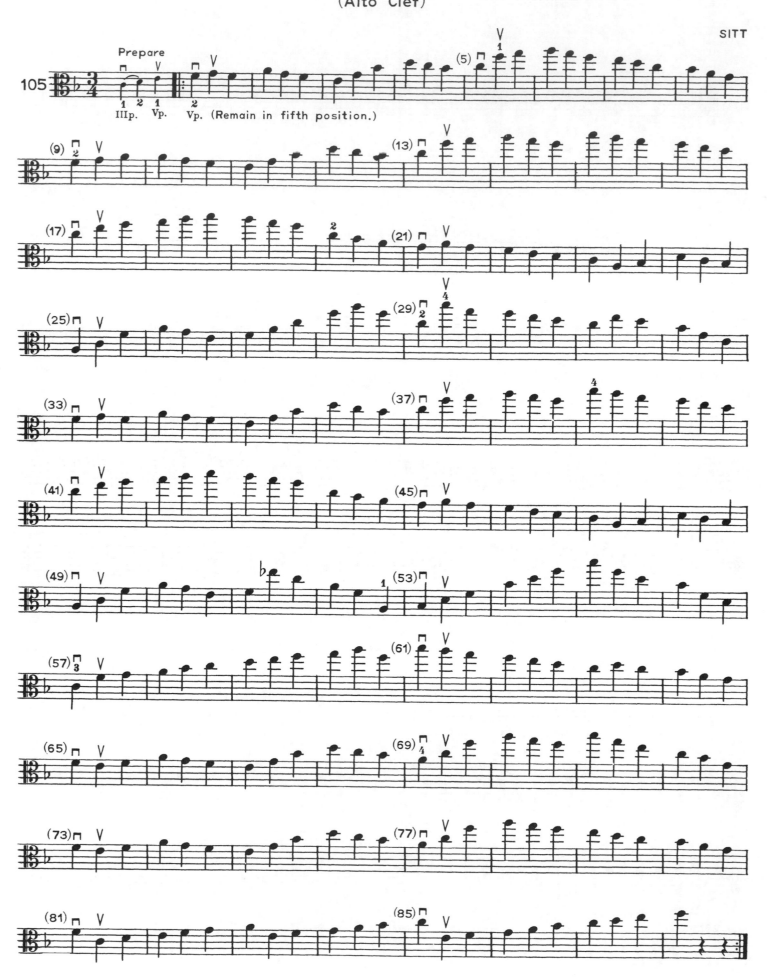

Fifth Position Etude in F Major
(Treble Clef)

SITT

Key of B♭ Major

Etude

DE BERIOT

Fingering High Tones
(Alto and Treble Clefs)

CAMPAGNOLI

EXERCISE

SPOHR

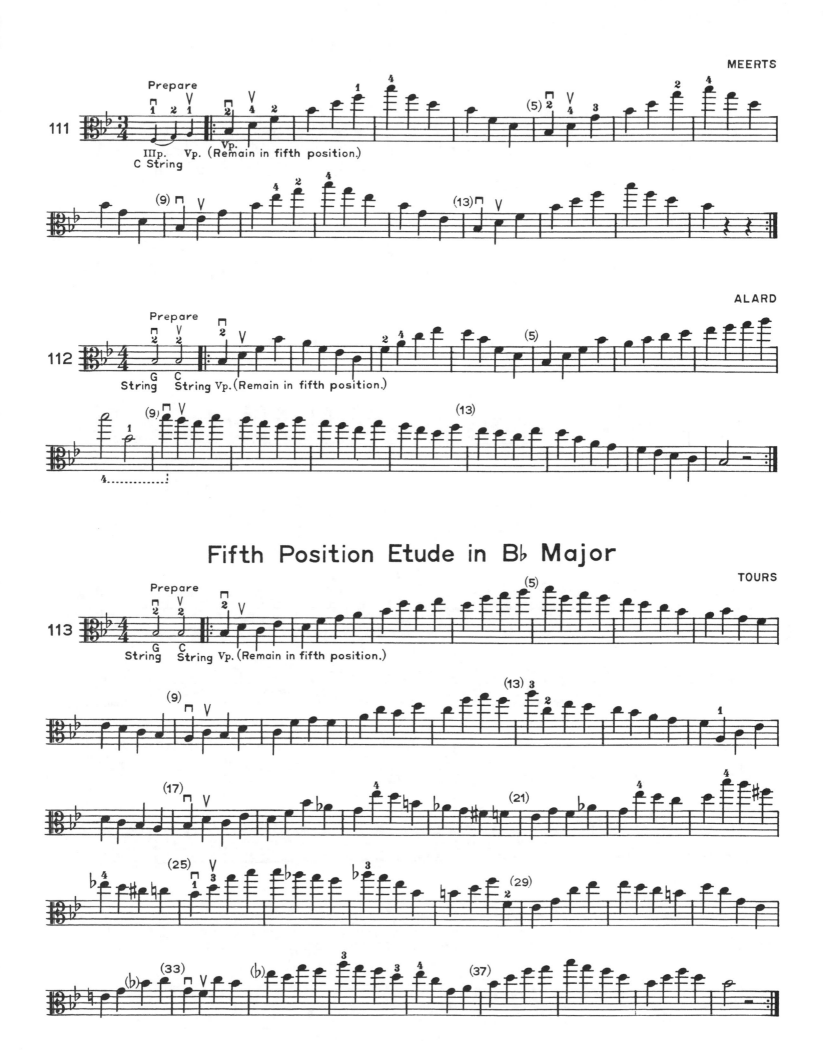

Fifth Position Etude in B♭ Major

Key of C Major

Fifth Position Etude in C Major

KAYSER

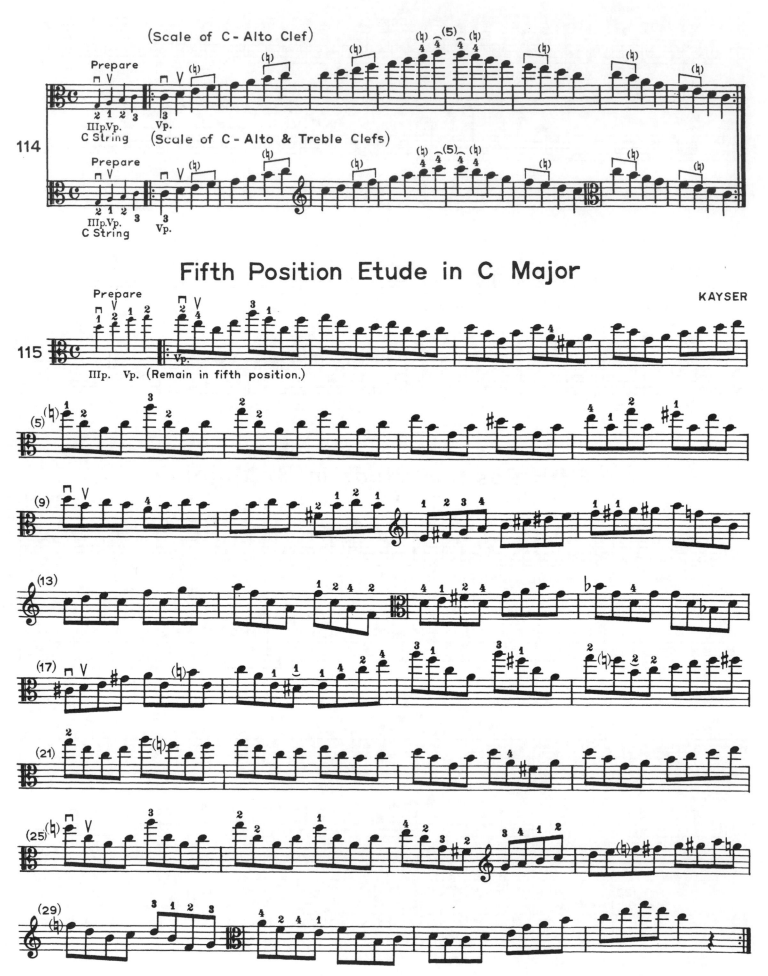

38

Key of G Major

EXERCISE

DE BERIOT

Fifth Position Etude in G Major

KAYSER

Key of D Major

119

Fifth Position Etude in D Major

RIES

Key of A Major

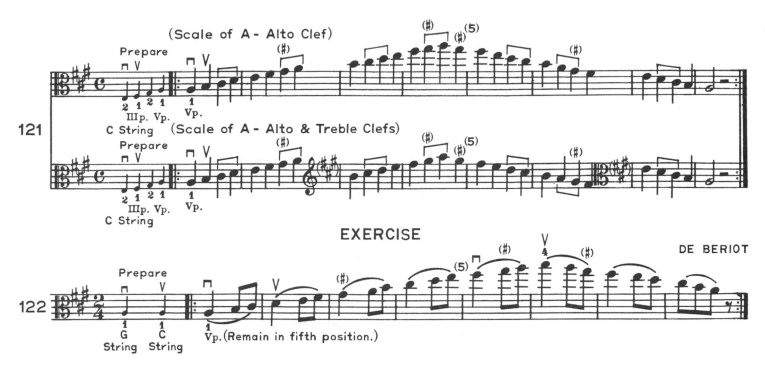

(Scale of A - Alto Clef)

121

C String (Scale of A - Alto & Treble Clefs)

EXERCISE

DE BERIOT

122

Vp. (Remain in fifth position.)

Fifth Position Etude in A Major

SITT

123

Vp. (Remain in fifth position.)

Key of Eb Major

EXERCISE

DE BERIOT

TECHNICAL STUDY

ALARD

Fifth Position Etude in Eb Major

KAYSER

Combined Positions
Shifting from First to Third to Fifth Position

The student should remember to shift forward on the finger that was last down, and likewise, to shift backward on the finger that was last down.

The student also should remember that the small notes in the exercises below merely indicate the movement of the fingers in shifting, and as the ability to shift from one note to another is perfected, the small notes eventually should not be heard.

ALARD

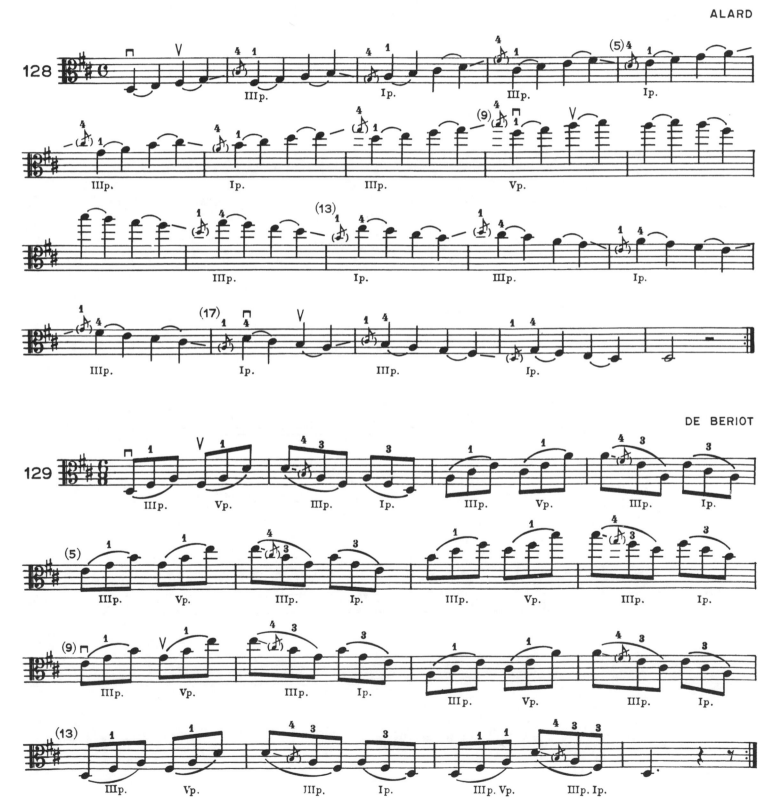

DE BERIOT

Shifting from Third to Fifth Position

A String

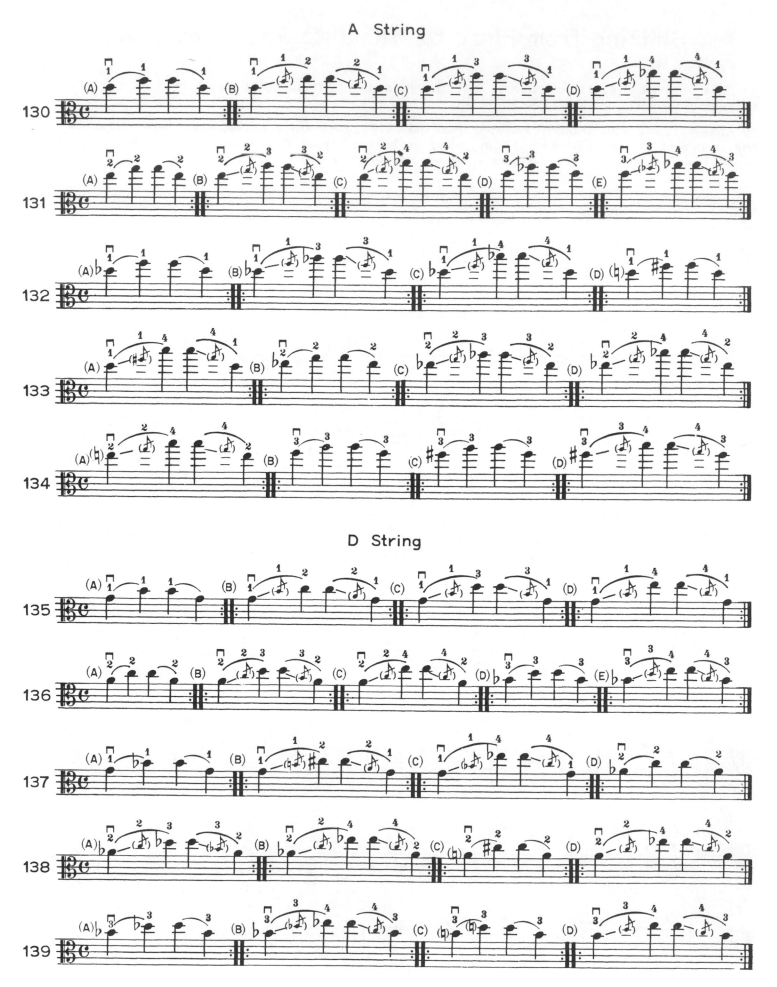

D String

G String

C String

Shifting Etude No. 1

DE BERIOT

Shifting Etude No. 2

MAZAS

Ševčík Exercises for Shifting the Position
From Third to Fifth Positions

Drink to Me Only with Thine Eyes

OLD ENGLISH BALLAD

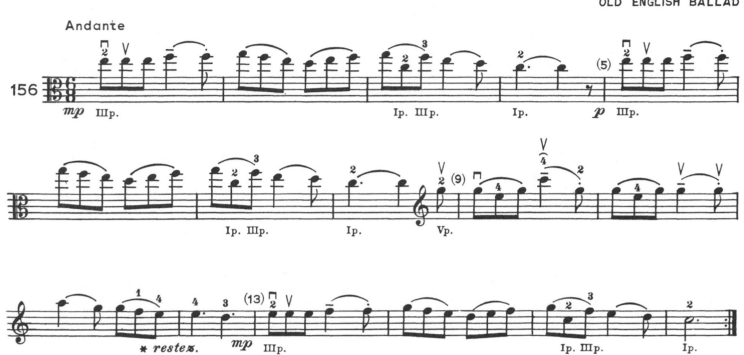

Swanee River

STEPHEN C. FOSTER

✻ *restez.* = Remain in position. Do not go to a lower position which has a similar fingering.

On Wings of Song

Andante tranquillo

O God, As Divers Aches of Heart

BACH

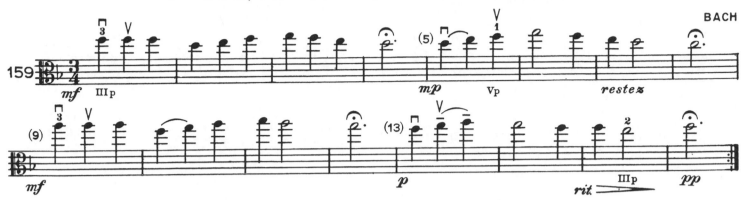

Praise Ye the Lord of Hosts
from "The Christmas Oratorio"

SAINT-SAENS

Thy Name We Hail
from "The Redemption"

GOUNOD

Lord and Master

BACH

Róndo Elégante
(DUET)

KREUTZER
Transcribed by
H. A. Hummel

Fantaisie Brillante
(DUET)

LEONARD
Transcribed by
H. A. Hummel

Advanced Shifting Etude
(Through Five Positions)

SITT

Fantaisie-Caprice
(Concert Etude in Five Positions)

DE BERIOT